Cockapoos as Pets

The Ultimate Guide for Cockapoos

Cockapoos General Info, Purchasing, Care, Cost, Keeping, Health, Supplies, Food, Breeding and More Included!

By Lolly Brown

Copyrights and Trademarks

All rights reserved. No part of this book may be reproduced or transformed in any form or by any means, graphic, electronic, or mechanical, including photocopying, recording, taping, or by any information storage retrieval system, without the written permission of the author.

This publication is Copyright ©2017 NRB Publishing, an imprint. Nevada. All products, graphics, publications, software and services mentioned and recommended in this publication are protected by trademarks. In such instance, all trademarks & copyright belong to the respective owners. For information consult www.NRBpublishing.com

Disclaimer and Legal Notice

This product is not legal, medical, or accounting advice and should not be interpreted in that manner. You need to do your own due-diligence to determine if the content of this product is right for you. While every attempt has been made to verify the information shared in this publication, neither the author, neither publisher, nor the affiliates assume any responsibility for errors, omissions or contrary interpretation of the subject matter herein. Any perceived slights to any specific person(s) or organization(s) are purely unintentional.

We have no control over the nature, content and availability of the web sites listed in this book. The inclusion of any web site links does not necessarily imply a recommendation or endorse the views expressed within them. We take no responsibility for, and will not be liable for, the websites being temporarily unavailable or being removed from the internet.

The accuracy and completeness of information provided herein and opinions stated herein are not guaranteed or warranted to produce any particular results, and the advice and strategies, contained herein may not be suitable for every individual. Neither the author nor the publisher shall be liable for any loss incurred as a consequence of the use and application, directly or indirectly, of any information presented in this work. This publication is designed to provide information in regard to the subject matter covered.

Neither the author nor the publisher assume any responsibility for any errors or omissions, nor do they represent or warrant that the ideas, information, actions, plans, suggestions contained in this book is in all cases accurate. It is the reader's responsibility to find advice before putting anything written in this book into practice. The information in this book is not intended to serve as legal, medical, or accounting advice.

Foreword

Cockapoos are one of those dogs that are quite the "usual type" at first – mainly because of their fun attitude, fluffy coats, has a suitable size, great for keepers and newbies alike, and just a generally free – spirited, active, and friendly looking pet making it great companions for families. However, their outgoing personality is just the tip of the iceberg because this designer breed is also a therapeutic dog – they are sensitive and intuitive to people's feelings. And they possess that sort of a hustle kind of attitude with an appropriate level of demeanor if they are raised up and trained right.

In this book, you'll be guided on how to keep them as pets, how to train them, provide the things they need, and also make them feel part of your life and family so that you can also feel at home with their company. Prepare for one heaven and hell of an adventure with this breed!

Table of Contents

Introduction 1

Chapter One: Cockapoos Inside Out! 5

    Physical Characteristics and General Qualities 6

    Behavior and Temperament 9

        Quick Facts 10

Chapter Two: Cockapoos as Pets 13

    Questions to Consider Before Keeping Cockapoos as Pets 14

    Understanding Your Cockapoo's Behavior 20

Chapter Three: Finding a Reputable Breeder 23

    Finding a Reputable Breeder 24

    What's the difference between a Licensed Breeder and a Hobby Breeder? 25

    Questions for Potential Breeders 30

Chapter Four: Puppy Preparation 35

    Housing Preparation 36

    Reminders for the Toilet Area 40

    Litter Training for Puppies 41

    Dog – Proofing Your Cockapoo 43

Chapter Five: Entertaining and Socializing Your Cockapoo 47

    Games for Your Cockapoos 48

Socialization Tips for Cockapoos 51

Cockapoo Training Basics 52

Chapter Six: Coat Types and Grooming 57

Different Cockapoo Coat Types 58

Grooming Your Cockapoo 60

Washing Your Pet 62

Chapter Seven: Feeding Your Cockapoo 65

Feeding and Nutrition 66

Understanding Dog Food labels 67

Nutritional Terms 70

What is a BARF Diet? 72

FAQs about Dog Feeding 74

Chapter Eight: Breeding Your Cockapoos 77

Reasons for Breeding 78

Reasons for Not Considering Becoming a Breeder 79

Other Factors to Consider 82

Breeding Basics 83

Chapter Nine: Health and Safety 85

Winter Care for Cockapoos 86

Christmas Hazards 89

Summer Care for Cockapoos 92

Chapter Ten: Care Sheet and Summary 97

Glossary of Dog Terms	109
Photo Credits	115
References	117

Introduction

Cockapoo is a designer dog bred from a Cocker Spaniel and a poodle. They have become increasingly popular mainly because of its affectionate and super friendly personalities. It's also perhaps because of their practical small to medium size and soft coats. This breed, however, may need regular grooming because otherwise, their furs can become kinked or matted if it's not looked after properly.

Introduction

There are many variations of the cockapoo due to crosses from different size poodles with a working, show or standard spaniels. These factors will surely influence their size, temperament factors, personality, and coat/skin. For example, if you cross a toy or miniature size poodle with a spaniel you can create a small cockapoo; if you bred it with a working spaniel cross, the cockapoo will tend to have a straighter hair/coat with higher levels of energy.

Many people are drawn to the cockapoos because they are generally a fun dog for people of all ages making them ideal as family companions. They are smart, affectionate, and fun which is why lots of keepers find them easy to train. Even if they only receive little training or guidance, they can easily pick up the instructions and learn lots of tricks.

Puppy cockapoos have a reputation for being too friendly; they're known for jumping up at people but sometimes can get distracted if they're playing with other dog which is why socializing them, teaching them appropriate greetings and focus at a young age is also important.

Much like children, cockapoos can be quite vocal especially when they're having fun with people or other pets. They also carry their playful side even as they become

Introduction

adults, so you can safely assume that they are quite young – at – hearts even if they reached their old age.

What most first time keepers don't know is that these dogs are one of the most sensitive breed of dogs, they are intuitive to people's emotions making them great dogs for people undergoing therapy or those who suffered from traumatizing experiences.

Cockapoos are active dogs who love to play and they're also commonly motivated by treats and even toys! Their high energy level makes them perfect pets for sporty people but don't worry even if you're not the sporty type, you can still have fun watching them show off their athletic abilities through different kinds of agility tests. These dog activities are great for bonding as well as mental stimulation – not to mention physical exercise for your cockapoo and for you! (obviously because you have to accompany them during their "dog agility training"). Find out more about them on the next chapters and learn what it takes to keep these active dogs as pets!

Introduction

Chapter One: Cockapoos Inside Out!

As if it's not been stressed enough, owning a dog is a huge commitment but it's also a joyful privilege. Even though you think you can fulfill the basic needs of your pet, there are still other things to consider as what you'll see in the next few chapters. In this chapter, we'll give you many reasons why cockapoos can be a perfect fit for your family. You'll learn their origin, history, and biological information as well as their usual behavior and temperament with people and other pets in general.

Chapter One: Cockapoos Inside Out!

Physical Characteristics and General Qualities

Cockapoodles or cockapoos made its debut around the 1950s when hobbyists and breeders decided that they want to create a low shedding dog. Today, cockapoos are one of the most popular designer dogs because of its loyal nature and charming looks! Since these dogs are a crossbreed of an American/English Cocker Spaniel and a poodle, they come in all sorts of sizes, colors and coat types. Some cockapoos inherit the traits of the Cocker Spaniel while some possess a poodle characteristic whether it's physical traits or behavioral temperaments. It all depends on how these dogs turn out but either way, they're perfect family pets.

They are very playful and affectionate making them sturdy enough to play fetch with children and at the same time cuddly enough to crawl on your lap for a warm and relaxing nap while you watch the TV or just chill outside. They form great bond with the family and loves to be around people all the time!

As mentioned earlier, they are exceptionally athletic and smart dogs making them easy to train. In fact, most first time keepers are shock because they quickly pick up the things they have been taught and also respond to commands. According to many breeders, cockapoo pups

Chapter One: Cockapoos Inside Out!

already know how to sit, stand, come, behave and do a few dog tricks in just six months. They are surely an intelligent designer breed because it is something that they got from their parents, both cocker spaniel dogs and poodles are two of the most clever dog breeds as well, no wonder why their offspring are like this. Although, these hyper dogs can be satisfied with just a simple walk around the park, you as the keeper should give time for them to exercise and let them run loose with other pets every now and then. A fence, spacious yard or a secured play area is necessary for them to exert all that energy.

The only downside is that the AKC or American Kennel Club which is the leading organization for dog breeds does not recognize the cockapoo as a breed since they mostly accept purebred dogs but rest assured that hobbyists and breeders overtime will continue to improve the breed. The good news is that cockapoos are recognized by several dog organizations, registries, and clubs in United States, in Europe and other parts of the world such as the following:

- The American K9 Hybrid Club
- Designer Breed Registry
- North American Cockapoo Registry
- Cockapoo Club of America
- International Designer K9 Registry
- Designer Dogs Kennel Club
- American Cockapoo Club
- Cockapoo Club of Great Britain

Chapter One: Cockapoos Inside Out!

Cockapoos are low shedder dogs but you have to keep their coats groomed up at least once a week. A bit of vacuum, trimming and styling is required to maintain their beautiful coats.

Adult cockapoos depending on their size weigh around 6 – 19 lbs. They can be classified as miniature (13 – 18 lbs.) and maxi cockapoos (19 lbs.), toy (7 – 12 lbs.), and also teacup breed (less than 6 lbs.) which is kind of similar to the different poodle types. When it comes to their height, Maxi or Standard Cockapoo can reach 15 inches; Mini cockapoos are typically 11 to 14 inches tall; Teacups only stand less than 10 inches while toy breeds is between 10 and 11 inches tall. They come in different colors like Black, Sable, Parti, Chocolate, Phantom, Buff, Roan, Apricot, White, Red, and Cream plus other range of colors depending of course on the parent breeds/hybrids.

Most cockapoos are healthier than their parent breeds because it doesn't have genetic defects that are often found in cocker spaniel and poodles. Although, they are generally healthy, they are still predispose to minor illnesses like ear infections (due to their dropped ears), parasites, cataracts, knee dislocation and other internal diseases.

Cockapoos live anywhere between 14 and 18 years, so it's quite a long term commitment for you as a keeper. If you want your pet to last this long, be sure to properly care for them by feeding them high quality food, providing appropriate shelter, meeting their exercise needs and spending quality time with them.

Behavior and Temperament

Cockapoos have tons of energy so better put it to good use by engaging him/her in several dog activities that will enhance their agility and strength to keep them stay healthy, active and stimulated. They're quite easy to train because they want to impress their owners and please you!

Most cockapoos love to play and they are extremely motivated by food which can be very suitable during training. They are very sociable not just with humans but with other dogs as well. They would really appreciate interaction and lots of play time outside with their own kin. If you're going to buy a cockapoo, it is important to make sure that their parents are working breeds because this will have an impact on your puppies' personality, energy, and temperament.

As mentioned earlier, it's important to train them at an early age especially when it comes to approaching people and other dogs as cockapoos usually gets very excited which can sometimes lead to inappropriate behaviors such as jumping, rough play and barking. Due to their personalities, cockapoos can get quite destructed in busy environments or whenever he/she is around other dogs which can become an issue especially during training. This is actually something to think about if you think you don't have much time in teaching these dogs some new and "proper" tricks, although if you become consistent in training, they can be fun, loyal and obedient dogs.

Quick Facts

Origin: United States

Pedigree: crossbreed of American/English Cocker Spaniel and Poodle

Breed Size/Type: Maxi, Mini, Toy and Teacup breed

Body Type and Appearance: These dogs have relatively small and broad heads have dropped ears that are small, well - set and furry, and they are available in many colors.

Height: Maxi or Standard Cockapoo can reach 15 inches; Mini cockapoos are typically 11 to 14 inches tall; Teacups only stand less than 10 inches while toy breeds is between 10 and 11 inches tall.

Weight: They can be classified as miniature (13 – 18 lbs.) and maxi cockapoos (19 lbs.), toy (7 – 12 lbs.), and also teacup breed (less than 6 lbs.) which is kind of similar to the different poodle types.

Chapter One: Cockapoos Inside Out!

Coat Length: around 4 – 6 inches of either flat, straight, wavy or poodle like coat

Coat Texture: dense, silky, soft fur

Color: Black, Sable, Parti, Chocolate, Phantom, Buff, Roan, Apricot, White, Red, and Cream plus other range of colors.

Ears: dropped ears, small

Tail: short to medium - length

Temperament: sociable, friendly, trainable, obedient, active, playful, loyal, affectionate

Strangers: super friendly around strangers

Other Dogs: generally loves to play with other dogs if properly trained and socialized

Other Pets: friendly with other pets including cats

Training: intelligent, obedient, and easily trained

Exercise Needs: regular amount of exercise is needed

Health Conditions: maybe prone minor illnesses like ear infections (due to their dropped ears), parasites, cataracts, knee dislocation and other internal diseases. .

Lifespan: average 14 – 18 years

Chapter One: Cockapoos Inside Out!

Chapter Two: Cockapoos as Pets

Just like any dogs or household pets, Cockapoo is surely a wonderful pet to keep. These cute creatures can enrich people's lives in many ways but things should still be considered especially if you want to acquire this particular breed. Before finding a reputable breeder, it's probably best to consider the questions provided in this chapter for you to be able to make an honest decision if cockapoo can fit your family, your personality and your lifestyle. This chapter will make you ponder on things that come with keeping this kind of dog.

Chapter Two: Cockapoos as Pets

Questions to Consider Before Keeping Cockapoos as Pets

Here are some things you need to consider before taking the next step. Make sure you read through this to see if this is the dog breed for you.

Can you provide long term commitment?

As mentioned earlier cockapoos can become your loving companion for a maximum of 18 years (or maybe more), so the first question you need to really to have a clear answer to is, can you commit in keeping them and providing for all their basic needs and wants? Basically, you have to spend money on food, shelter, grooming, and other necessities but you also have to spend time and energy playing around with them and making them feel loved and appreciated just like another member of the family. You have to do this every day for the rest of your dog's life! If you have an active social life or you're someone who's not around the house all the time, cockapoos may not be the ideal dog for you.

Do you have patience to train them?

Cockapoos are pretty easy to train but they can still require a lot of effort on your part especially when they're

Chapter Two: Cockapoos as Pets

young. Just like kids, you have to care for them, understand their behavior, be patient with them and even build a routine for them so that they can settle and feel "at home" with your company. Aside from basic training, one of the hardest parts is housebreaking and potty/toilet training. You have to constantly and consistently follow up on them so that the 'rules' can be inculcated in their minds which can foster good behavior. You also have to aid them if they're going through their different transitions in life, from their puppy years to their juvenile years until they reach adulthood. As a keeper, patience it needed if you want them to have and maintain their discipline.

Grooming and coat maintenance can cost a lot; do you have the budget and time?

In order to keep their coats from becoming matted, you'll need to groom them regularly especially when they reached adulthood. They'll usually require regular combing and trimming. If you choose not to do it yourself, you can have the option of bringing them to a professional pet groomer which of course can be quite costly and you have to set a schedule for it as well. Most cockapoos love to roll around in the ground, muds and water, making their coats, paws, and body dry and dirty. Moreover, if things like twigs or grass seeds get attached to your cockapoo's coats it can be hard to remove and may require a vet to perform the removing procedure because these things can be painful for your dog. Grooming also means doing a daily routine to check if their coat is still in good condition after playing outside so make sure you have time for it.

Can you keep up with their energy?

Cockapoos' energy levels are off the charts! You have to make sure that they get enough mental and physical stimulation by taking them out for walks, letting them run around the yard, letting them play with other dogs or by simply entertaining by playing games, training and tricks as well as doing dog obstacles. They are super active so make sure that you can keep up with their energy.

Can you cover possible health treatments or can you avail a pet insurance?

Although cockapoos are generally healthy, they can still get sick from time to time. You may need to have them checked every month or so by the vet to do a routine checkup to make sure that they're in good health which can of course cost you – not to mention if they do need treatment. Aside from that, you should be able to set aside a certain amount to avail the needed vaccines or puppy shots for them.

Chapter Two: Cockapoos as Pets

Availing of pet insurance is optional but it's a good option in cases of emergency because it can cover the expenses of medical treatments as well as the accidents that can be caused by your dog. However, illnesses like flea and worming treatments, spaying/neutering and even routine checkups are not usually covered so you have to pay for those things. Make sure you set aside a certain amount for these cases.

Cockapoos craves attention; can you give them your full commitment?

These dogs are not the independent type unlike other kinds of breeds. In fact, they're sort of 'clingy' pets and it's safe to say that they are suckers for attention! They are people pleaser and will do anything just to make you focus on them which is why they can also be prone to separation anxiety especially if they have already formed closed bonds with your family. So if you think you can't do that, better get them use to being not so attached at an early age.

Do you want a cockapoo because you've been told that they are hypoallergenic?

Even if cockapoos have hypoallergenic traits that they got from their parent breeds, it doesn't mean that they're completely allergic free, it only means that compared to normal dog breeds, they have less dander. People with allergies can still suffer from allergic reaction due to the dog's skin and saliva, and not just because of their coat.

Since cockapoos are not entirely poodle breeds, there's no guarantee that they would have the traits of being a low molting coat such as those found in poodle breeds. Make sure that before you get a cockapoo, ask the breeder if you can interact with them over a period of time to check if you won't get any allergic reactions.

Do you just want a cockapoo because they don't molt or just because they are cute?

There's no guarantee that they will fully acquire the traits of their poodle parent breed, so expect that they can also shed some hair. They still molt but they're not heavy molters.

Don't just look at their free – spirited and charming appearance; you have to also factor in if you can handle their temperaments and personality – not to mention all their needs. Before getting a dog, identify your purpose first and probably have a much deeper intention than just keeping them for keeping's sake. Remember, they are just like babies, you can't just return them if you find them annoying or whatnot.

Chapter Two: Cockapoos as Pets

Do you want a cockapoo because you think they are classy?

Cockapoos are cute and rugged, so if you are a classy type of person with a finesse behavior, then this dog is not for you as they can be very active and one who loves to get their paws dirty all the time. They are loyal and obedient dogs that can be silenced from time to time but a classy attitude is not in their vocabulary.

Do you want a cockapoo because you think they don't get sick?

Just like other dogs, they are pre-disposed to certain illnesses. So if you want to lessen the risk, you may need to test them if they're clear from genetic diseases before acquiring them. Make sure that you are aware of its possible health condition and how they are raised to minimize trips to the vet.

Can you spend time with them even if you work full time?

Many people who own a cockapoo have full time jobs but as a potential keeper you need to consider how long your pet will be left alone the house especially while they are still young pups until their juvenile years because this is the time when they will need you the most. As they grow and develop, they need to be properly fed, routinely checked and consistently trained. You can't also leave them for a very long period of time; you may need to ask help from a friend or family member to look after the pet if you're going to have a vacation. Time and attention is really important for this breed.

Understanding Your Cockapoo's Behavior

The relationship between dogs and humans is remarkable and has been going on for so long that some scientists suggest dogs have affected human evolution just as we have quite clearly affected theirs. In the wild, dogs live in social groups which are hierarchical, with a dominant dog (usually a male) and its subordinates. These hierarchies are designed to prevent social discord by ensuring that everyone knows their place. In your home, it will come to see your family as its pack. Your pup must learn its place in the pecking order of your pack and that place must be at the bottom, the good news is that there are many painless ways of asserting your dominance over your dog.

A dog's behavior is a combination of instant and acquired or learned behavior and dogs go through developmental stages just as people do. Dogs must learn by trial and error, they try something – if the outcome is rewarding they are more likely to do it again – if the outcome is unpleasant they are less likely to do it again. The more often they have a pleasant outcome from a behavior the more rapidly they will learn to perform that behavior.

Chapter Two: Cockapoos as Pets

Chapter Three: Finding a Reputable Breeder

Now that you have learned what cockapoos are, their basic needs, characteristics, and probably have chosen the kind of size or color you want, it's now time to find you the right breeder. This next step is very important so that you can avoid purchasing from unscrupulous puppy breeders. Just like any consumer, you should take the time to really screen your potential seller before making the deal with them. As a golden rule, you should buy from someone who are not just breeding for the money but someone who are responsible, passionate, and loves their litters. This chapter will help you distinguish the bad, the good and the best cockapoo breeders.

Chapter Three: Finding A Reputable Breeder

Finding a Reputable Breeder

Recommendations from family, friends, and cockapoo keepers are great place to start. Like purchasing any kind of items, word of mouth is still the best marketing strategy and therefore the best place to begin your search. With the advent of the internet, you can easily ask and connect with people who have had previous experience buying from certain breeders. You can easily know if that local breeder is reputable by listening to what other people say about them. Your own vet can also recommend you with some local breeders that are trustworthy as well. At the end of the day though, people's recommendations are just base on their personal opinions or preferences and while they are important as part of your screening process, it's still up to you to have your own standards when it comes to finding the right breeder.

What you can do is to jot down the names of the recommended breeders and if possible, put in the best and worst comment you've received for that particular person. Then start researching how they are as a breeder and prove their reputation for yourself.

If you come across advertisements on social media or dog sites, you still have to do your own research and not just take their word for it. Sometimes the people behind the

Chapter Three: Finding A Reputable Breeder

advertisements that offer cheap prices are often used by puppy farmers or brokers to sell their breeds raised from illegal puppy mills. These puppy mills mostly produce sick puppies due to improper husbandry practices which are then sold to other breeders for an inexpensive price. You want to avoid those breeders because the puppies they're selling are surely unhealthy and may even infect your other pets if you brought them home.

You also want to avoid imported puppies especially if you're not sure where they've come from and how they were breed or raised. Asking questions related to how these puppies were raised, getting into specifics, and knowing the reason why they do what they do will make them reveal their intentions and true characteristics if they are trustworthy or reputable enough. With that being said here are some guidelines and questions to help you decide if the person you're going to get your puppy from is worth your time.

What's the difference between a Licensed Breeder and a Hobby Breeder?

Before we do any comparison, I just want to clarify that hobbyists/hobby breeders and licensed breeders are both legit and could potentially be reputable. And even if both of them has pros and cons, they can have a way better

Chapter Three: Finding A Reputable Breeder

reputation and track record than buying from unknown breeders or random pet ads online.

Hobby Breeders vs. Licensed Breeders

Hobbyists are people who are just really passionate about dogs or particular breeds of dogs that they have decided to bred on their own and eventually find new owners for their puppies, perhaps their only difference with licensed breeders is that they are not officially registered by any form of organization or registry or may not have an actual business. It's kind of like they're freelancing as a dog breeder but they're so passionate about it that they make sure they become reputable hobbyists.

When it comes to formally comparing the two, check out the following points below:

Hobby Breeder

- Hobbyists are not permitted to breed more than 4 litters in a year which is why availability of puppies can be restricted.

- The parent breeds of the puppies they sell are usually their own household pet which is why you can be assured that they've come from a good home. This is also the reason why the puppies they will breed will be kept in their homes and not placed in kennels.

- Most likely, hobbyists will mate their pet with other hobbyists because they might only own either a male or female dog but it doesn't apply to all hobby breeders. Some have a male and female breed.

Licensed Breeder

- Licensed breeders approved by a certain organization or someone who has been issued with a certificate can breed more than four litters in a year which means that they can have puppies all year round and that you are less likely to be put into the waiting list.

- Licensed breeders may sell or re-home their dogs when breeding time is over, this is because some breeders may not able to keep lots of their breeding dogs as pets. It allows them acquire a new breeding stock.

- Licensed breeders also have many breeding studs or bitches, and because they are operating in this way, they are keeping these pets in a separate kennel and not kept in their homes.

Chapter Three: Finding A Reputable Breeder

- Licensed breeders provides bitches and stud services

- Licensed breeders undergo inspection, have detailed records for each of their pets, and strictly follow the rules of not breeding bitches until they reach a year after their last whelping. Each bitch is also not allowed to have more than 6 litters in a year because it is in the contract.

Does this mean that if I acquire a dog from a licensed breeder, I can be guaranteed that I'll be protected because they are adhering to the rules/regulations?

Yes and no, sometimes the puppy farmers from puppy mills have licenses but it doesn't necessarily mean that they are reputable. This is the reason why you still have to do your own investigation if they are following good breeding practices. Being a licensed breeder is not a guarantee that they are considered as an ethical or responsible breeder. However, you can be protected if ever you got a sick puppy by filing a complaint against them through the registry or organization where they got their license so that their operation can be stopped or be subjected for inspection.

Chapter Three: Finding A Reputable Breeder

Should I instantly avoid puppies that are cheap?

Not necessarily, of course if you can get a discount you should, provided that the puppy is healthy and was raised by a reputable breeder. Price is not entirely an indication that a breed is of quality, sometimes it's based upon competition or the law of supply and demand. However, you should still be wary because if they priced the puppy way too low, perhaps below than the average, it could mean that the puppies may not be medically tested or they are not of quality.

Let's face it, breeding pets is an expensive hobby, so the pricing should at least be on average with their competitors (if any). With that being said, buying an expensive dog is also not a guarantee that it is of quality. Sometimes breeders are good with their marketing just to attract people in buying from them. They usually tell people that the color or characteristics of a certain breed is rare which is why they are charging a premium price for it but in reality, it's just like any other dog breed. A reputable breeder will charge their pups equally and not segregate which is "special" and which is not.

Chapter Three: Finding A Reputable Breeder

Questions for Potential Breeders

Questions to ask:

How old are the puppies (that they're going to sell to you)?
The answer should be at least 8 weeks or older.

Are the parents of dogs are healthy, can you prove it?
The answer is yes and they should have copy of health or medical certificates.

Can the parents of the pups be viewed?
You have to at least see the mom of the pups to check out if she was not overbred or is in poor condition. This is also to assure that the breeder is the one who bred the pups or if say, they used bitches/stud services (if the breeder is also reputable). You would want to assure that the pups are not from puppy brokers or unsanitary puppy mills. The mom should look healthy, and should look like she gave birth; you can see this if she shows interests in her offspring.

How old are the parents and how many litters did the mom produced this year?
The bitch should at least be two years old to make sure that they are matured already. For cocker spaniel moms, these dogs are much slower to mature which is why they shouldn't bred every season. Ideally, bitches should only

Chapter Three: Finding A Reputable Breeder

have at least 2 – 4 litters in their lifetime and they shouldn't be bred after reaching 6 years old.

Are the pups being regularly wormed?
The breeder should provide you with what kind of wormer was used and how frequent the puppies are undergoing the processed. Puppies should be wormed every two weeks until they hit 12 weeks old. From then on, until they are 6 month old, worming should be conducted monthly

Are the puppies vaccinated and treated for fleas?
Puppies should be vaccinated around 8 to 10 weeks old, sometimes depending on the recommendation of their vet. The breeder should provide you with a record of the vaccines that the puppy has received ever since they are born.

Are the puppies raised indoors?
This is to find out if the breeder/hobbyist have housebroken the puppy or have done some initial socialization practices around the house, to people and with other pets. If the puppies live in a kennel, ask the breeder if they have socialized the pups because it should be part of their development.

Chapter Three: Finding A Reputable Breeder

Are the puppies' microchipped?

The puppies should be registered and microchipped once they reached 8 weeks old. Microchipping is a process where a chip is surgically placed on the dog's skin. The chip contains the information of the dog and its owner so that if the pup gets lost, they can be scanned and returns back to their owners. Legit or responsible breeders should have their puppies' microchipped.

Do you offer after sale support?

If the breeder is responsible and reputable, he/she will still care for his/her puppies by being open to questions even after giving them to their new owners, and perhaps be willing to offer help through advice when it comes to raising their litter. He/she must also be willing to re-home the puppy if you won't be able to raise it for some reason.

Can you provide a contract?

This is another proof that the breeder is legit. However, not all breeders will give you a proof of sale, so you have to ask them the reason why they won't give you any contract. You should also ask if there's some sort of warranty, wherein if you found out that the puppy has some defects or health conditions, if you could get a refund for it and re-home it back to the breeder you should choose to.

Chapter Three: Finding A Reputable Breeder

Does the puppy have a free insurance?

Some breeders will give you an insurance that are free for the first four weeks, make sure that the plan is transferred to your name once you seal the deal and learn how to renew it or buy a dog insurance after it free insurance expires.

Will the puppy come home with a "puppy pack"?

A puppy pack is composed of the pup's toys, a blanket with their mom's scent, and pieces of advice by the breeder about the type of food, the medical records, and some important/necessary details for the puppy.

Do you require a deposit?

Most breeders do, so don't be surprise about it. And often times it is also non-refundable. So once you have put down a deposit, make sure that you're committed in buying from that breeder.

Notice if the breeder is also asking you questions.

A mark of a true and responsible breeder is if they ask you questions, so don't feel threaten because they just want to ensure that you're also a responsible keeper. They will usually ask you about your background, your lifestyle and some other personal information relevant to keeping a puppy. If they feel that you will take care of the puppies that they raised, both of you will have a great relationship.

Chapter Three: Finding A Reputable Breeder

Chapter Four: Puppy Preparation

Now that you have decided on whom you are going to buy from and you're probably just waiting for your puppy cockapoo to arrive, the next step is to prep up your home and your family for the coming of your new cute and cuddly member! This chapter will delve deeper on the housing requirements that your new pup needs along with the materials they'll require so that they can easily adjust in their new homes. We'll also give you some guidelines on how to dog proof your house to ensure that your new pet is safe if ever he/she tries to snoop around your house.

Chapter Four: Puppy Preparation

Housing Preparation

Below are the things you'll need to prepare while waiting for you cockapoo puppy.

Crate

The ideal crate size for puppy cockapoos is around 36 inches, this is to ensure that your puppy have an ample space where he/she can move around comfortably and sleep well. There are different kinds of crates that you can purchase online or in many stores; some have dividers in it wherein you can use one side as the space for its bed, while the other half could be the toilet area or the play area. The important thing is to place the crate in the familiar part of the house where it can be near you so you can supervise it. Avoid placing the crate in an isolated area.

You can set up the crate near the living room or probably near the couch where you hang out often. Make sure to also place it somewhere where he/she can peacefully rest – a location that is not too crowded or isolated from your family. To complete the set up, you can buy bed sheets or use the blanket that the breeder gave you because it has their mom's scent making them comfortable. Don't use the crate/cage as a punishment area if ever they misbehave, it should be their save haven and their go – to place where

Chapter Four: Puppy Preparation

they can have some "me" time. Keep in mind to remove the collars, tags or leash because it can easily get caught inside the cage and could cause injury or may even strangle your dog if it struggles to let go and free itself.

Bedding

You need not to spend a lot of money in buying a bed because they will surely outgrow it overtime, not to mention the fact that they could spend their time chewing most of it especially when they reached their teething stage. What we suggests you do is for you to save money is to grab an old cardboard box of some sort and just place a newspaper, a wool or a blanket over it. Of course, it's up to you if you wanted to buy more comfortable bedding. Many pet shops and online stores offer different designs and they could be made out of fabric, sofa or plastic.

Another popular type of bedding is called a vet bed because it's very easy to wash; it's cozy, soft, puppy proof and has variety of colors and designs that will surely make your cockapoo happy. You can also buy snuggle toys or a ticking clock wrapped up in some cloth to simulate their mom's heartbeat. These things have a realistic heartbeat and can also function as a warming pet that simulates another puppy and helps in comforting younger puppies to transition from their breeder to their new keepers. It's much useful during your pet's early days.

Chapter Four: Puppy Preparation

Puppy Pads

Puppy pads are optional but it can be of great help if you want your puppy to pee or poo in the appropriate toilet area. It's cheap and it could easily toilet train your puppy.

Toys

You should provide at least 3 or more dog toys to stimulate your cockapoo. Alternate the toys every week or every now and then or find out what toy your pet prefers. It's also best to supply a variety of toys serve for different purposes to keep your puppy interested. Always supervise your pets while he/she is playing its toys.

You can also buy chewing toys to satisfy your dog's instinct to chew and also relieve pressurized gums. There are also toys that you can buy to stimulate your dog's senses; these toys have varying colors, sounds, or smells. Rubber squeaky and puzzle toys can also be ideal because they are fun, noisy and also provide mental and physical stimulation especially for young pups.

Kitchen Roll

Kitchen roll is way cheaper than washing powders or other sort of chemical – based cleaners. They does the same job of removing the odor, removing urine and fecal smell if in case your puppy relieves itself in carpets or other areas in your home. Kitchen roll is used so that the urine or poo of your puppy will not retain its smell because if you don't clean it well, they'll smell the scent and is most likely to relive itself in that same inappropriate area.

Water Dishes and Food bowls

You need to provide your dog with water dishes, and food bowls especially if you're going away for a certain period of time. Most owners recommend a non – breakable, non – spill water bowl otherwise your puppy or dog will spill its water, and will be left with no water for days while you are away. You can also buy a ceramic or glass water/food bowls, however it is only ideal if you are at home because if in case the puppy breaks it, he/she might ingest the broken pieces or injure its food with the shattered glass. A stainless food and water dishes are also ideal because it's durable and also quite easy to clean. It's also safe for your pet, but it can be tipped over as well.

Poo Bags

You can buy cheap ones in the supermarket to segregate their poo in your garbage.

Chapter Four: Puppy Preparation

Reminders for the Toilet Area

- When setting up the pooping area inside your dog's crate, it should be located on the opposite side of your dog's sleeping area. You should make sure that the space is far away as possible from their crate or from where you are feeding them.

- If you have done some potty training already outside on the grass, and you want to train your pet to pee or poo inside its own play pen, you might want to consider buying a synthetic grass from your local hardware store. You might want to put the synthetic grass in a tray or buy a synthetic interlocking grass tiles.

- The synthetic interlocking grass tile is very ideal because it has drainage holes to prevent fluids from flowing; you just have to replace a puppy pee pad underneath it to soak up the excess fluids.

- Whenever you're cleaning the synthetic grass, you can just hose it down, and let it dry for a while. You can buy more than two square grasses so that you have a spare while you are drying the other set after cleaning it.

Chapter Four: Puppy Preparation

- The toileting sofa should be removed if you are at home, and should only be provided when you're away. The reason for this is that you want to avoid tolerating the puppy that it's okay to toilet indoors; ensure that your pet poo or pee outdoors at every possible opportunity to accelerate toilet training.

- A plastic airline create with a wire front door is an excellent aid in toilet training your dog and also provides a secure den for them to sleep in. Puppies resist soiling their beds, so it will rapidly learn to hold on overnight and the cage will allow you to take your puppy to where you want it to poo every morning - with the reasonable expectation that it will indeed go.

- Take your pup out before you go to bed, them put them to bed. Then take the puppy out to its toilet area first thing in the morning.

Litter Training for Puppies

Pups become house trained by developing a habit. It usually takes about two to four weeks of constant vigilance. You need to know a few facts about elimination behavior. Pups are most likely to defecate and urinate after sleep, after a meal or after exercise. When they are about to poo, they

Chapter Four: Puppy Preparation

will sniff the ground and may walk in circles; there may also be a little warning before they urinate. They will try very hard not to wee and poo in their own beds unless they are confined too long. Once they have started using one place they are likely to keep using it because of the smell, your cockapoo will have preferred toilet places which are why they will often seek out a carpet.

As soon as you get home on your first day, take your pup to the designated place in your garden and wait there patiently until they relieve themselves. From then on take your pup outside, to the place you have chosen, as soon as it wakes up in the morning, after a sleep, after a meal, and whenever it begins to walk around sniffing the ground and at least every two hours throughout the day. If it urinates or poops in the designated toilet area, make sure to praise him/her or give it a food reward this way it could have a positive reinforcement.

If you catch your pup in the act inside the house just firmly say no, pick it up, and take it to the place you have chosen for it to use. If you are too late clean up the mess, use soap and water and then an enzymatic cleanser to get rid of the smell so that your cockapoo will not relieve themselves in that area again. As mentioned earlier, a freight cage – a plastic shell with a wire front door – is a great tool that most newbie keepers use to do toilet training.

Your pup will hold on as long as possible rather than poop in its bed and a couple of nights should be enough to train it to sleep through. Take it out last thing at night and first thing in the morning and you will have control over its elimination behavior at least once each morning. If your cockapoo make a mess inside the house or its cage, don't punish your puppy because it could affect its behavior even more.

Puppies cannot make the connection that there's a poop on the rug and your angry about it. Never rub its nose in it – the pup will have no idea whatsoever why you are doing this and will not learn from the experience. If you are careful and really take the time to discipline your dog, he/she should be house trained in about two weeks or in just a month.

Dog – Proofing Your Cockapoo

Protect your pup from various household hazards to eliminate any unwanted accidents or situations by dog proofing your house. This should be done before your pet arrives or before you take them home. Check out the tips below:

- Provide fences, a screened porch or a safe enclosure. Be sure to dog-proof your yard so that your dog

Chapter Four: Puppy Preparation

could experience the outdoors safely.

- Remove any poisonous plants since dogs are naturally curious, and likes to chew anything. If your dog chew any plants, even the non-poisonous ones can cause vomiting and diarrhea or fatality.

- Install padded perches indoors near a window frame or in your patio so that your pet could enjoy and hang out but do not leave your doors and screens unlocked.

- Do not leave your appliances plugged, as mentioned earlier, they will chew anything including electric wires, not only is this potentially fatal for your dog but also a dangerous threat for your home.

- Buy a harness and train your dog to walk on a leash when going around the neighborhood.

- Consider buying a ready-made dog tree to provide climbing opportunities for your dog inside.

- Make sure to keep lots of dog toys out and put anything precious and destructible away.

Chapter Four: Puppy Preparation

- Make sure to keep away toxic liquids or materials like cleaning supplies or other household items that can harm them.

- Make sure that your puppy will not be able to enter bathrooms or kitchens alone because it can be dangerous for them.

- Once your dog arrives, you can observe it as it explores and become familiar with your home, you'll and also get to discover some things you need to dog – proof.

Chapter Five: Entertaining and Socializing Your Cockapoo

One of the joys of having a pet is the fact that you have something to play with! A living, moving creature that you can count on when you're down, that you can smooch with kisses and cuddle anytime, and someone that really connects with you in an emotional way as if they were real human beings. Dogs and even other pets in general give nothing but joy to the family which is why we love them as one of our own. This chapter will surely be a great read because you'll learn some tips on the kinds of games you can play with your pet to keep them fit and stimulated. You'll

Chapter Five: Entertaining and Training Your Cockapoo

also learn how to train and socialize them so that they can serve as a bundle of joy to your family and others.

Games for Your Cockapoos

You can keep your cockapoo stimulated by teaching him some good old dog tricks like "High Five," "Play Dead," or "Give Paw." As previously mentioned, this designer breed is quick to learn especially if he is rewarded with treats and love from his keeper. You can check out many kinds of dog tricks online if you're serious about teaching your dog some cool moves. If you want to take it up a notch and solidify your bonding with one another, you can both take "Dancing with Dogs" classes wherein dogs are taught several moves and tricks while being in sync with you and the music! This will surely teach him discipline and obedience while being physically and mentally stimulated. The bonus is that they get to have fun with you and you get to enjoy time with your pet cockapoo as well.

Here are some things you can do to keep your dog entertained outside and inside the house and during rainy days:

Hide The Treat!

Obviously, it won't be like your typical hide and seek – they'd find you every time through their sniffing abilities!

Chapter Five: Entertaining and Training Your Cockapoo

Instead of hiding yourself, this is a game where you hide their food! Once you bought treats like kibbles or other dog friendly food that your puppy likes, you can either throw it in the garden for them find it or simply tuck it away in some sort of cube to keep them occupied. During summer time what you can do to "break the ice" is to literally put the treats and freeze it up in ice and see how they get it. Another fun option is to roll up the treats in a towel or place it in a tray and just hide them around the house for him to find. These are good activities to enhance your dog's scent or smell skills plus it somewhat teach them that they have to work hard when it comes to finding their food!

Blow Up that Balloon!

What you can do is to tether a balloon or attach a string to a small ball then just hang it up in a ceiling fan or attach it somewhere where they can't reach it. This will enhance your dog's agile abilities because he'll have fun trying to get the balloon or that ball. This may be suitable for cockapoos that have that persistent attitude. This activity could wear out your dog so make sure to supervise them as they play or only give a certain period of time to do this activity.

Sand Pit

Chapter Five: Entertaining and Training Your Cockapoo

If you have just a small yard what you can do is to set up a sandbox and fill it with sand or soil and then bury some treats or toys so that your dog can sniff and dig through them.

Trick or Treats?

What you can do while your cockapoo is watching is to get one or two boxes that have different size and color then put a toy/treat in one of the two boxes. After doing just cover the box with a lid or a cloth and then move the boxes around and let him figure out which one has the treat. This can also be used for dexterity training where your dog needs to open the boxes.

Puzzle Box

Just fill a cardboard box with treats and crumpled newspaper then slightly close the box and put a few holes in it so that your pet can smell the treat and attract him to play around or destroy the box to get the treats.

Bubbles

Just purchase cheap bubble makers that are non-toxic or buy an automatic one and just let them pop the bubbles around your yard

Chapter Five: Entertaining and Training Your Cockapoo

Swimming

If you have a pool or an inflatable pool, then take your cockapoo for a swim. Play fetch with them by throwing it out into the water so that your dog can have fun and keep him stimulated. This is perfect during summer or humid days.

Bobbing Balls

Another fun activity that your cockapoo will surely love is called bobbing balls. This is quite similar with apple bobbing done in parties. Just get a relatively deep tub, fill it up with water and place the plastic balls/apples in it so that when they try to bite it, because the water is deep, it will slip up and they'll go bobbing under the water to just grab the ball/fruit.

Socialization Tips for Cockapoos

Socialization is essential for puppies when they are young because the experiences they have during this impressionable period will determine who they are as an adult. That's why the first few weeks of your cockapoo's life are incredibly important. If your puppy isn't properly

Chapter Five: Entertaining and Training Your Cockapoo

socialized, he might turn into a wary adult dog who responds to new people and unfamiliar situations with fear or uncertainty which is why you should follow the socialization tips given below:

- Mingle your puppy to different kinds of people by introducing your puppy to friends in the comfort of your own home where your puppy feels safe. You can also take your dog with you to the pet store or to a friend's house so that it experiences new locations.

- Introduce your puppy to children of different ages. Just supervise the kids to make sure they handle the puppy safely. Take your puppy with you in the car when you run errands, make them part of your daily routine as much as possible.

- You should also expose your cockapoo to various appliances and tools around the house as well as outside your neighborhood so that he can hear loud noises and get used to it.

Cockapoo Training Basics

Different methods of training hinges on your dog's natural desire to please you so in essence, you train your dog

Chapter Five: Entertaining and Training Your Cockapoo

to repeat desired behaviors by rewarding him for doing them. For example, if you want your dog to sit when you command them to, you have to teach him what the command means and then reward him each time he responds to the command appropriately.

The key to success with positive reinforcement training lies in helping your dog to identify the desired behavior using a clicker. You go through the normal process of training, giving your dog a command and guiding him to perform the desired behavior. Then, as soon as he displays the behavior you click the clicker and immediately issue a reward – this helps your dog to learn more quickly which behavior it is that you desire. You should only use the clicker during the first few repetitions of a training sequence until your dog learns what the desired behavior is because you don't want him to become dependent on the clicker to perform that behavior.

Another method you can use is punishment – but not the violent kind of punishment. This type of training is almost the opposite of positive reinforcement training – rather than rewarding your dog for performing desired behaviors, you punish him for performing unwanted behaviors. It doesn't involved hurting your pet or not feeding him for a day just give your dog the opposite of what he wants to curb the negative behavior in question. This type of training is sometimes effective as a method for curbing negative behaviors.

Chapter Five: Entertaining and Training Your Cockapoo

Dog training involves things like never letting the dog walk through the door before you, or waiting to feed your dog until after you have eaten. Dogs are pack animals, which is why they adapt so well to human society. They are adapted to cope with a complex set of relationships. The relationship between dogs and humans is remarkable and has been going on for so long that some scientists suggest dogs have affected human evolution just as we have quite clearly affected theirs.

In the wild, dogs live in social groups which are hierarchical, with a dominant dog and its subordinates. These hierarchies are designed to prevent social discord by ensuring that everyone knows their place. In your home, it will come to see your family as its pack. Your pup must learn its place in the pecking order of your pack and that place must be at the bottom, the good news is that there are many painless ways of asserting your dominance over your dog.

A dog's behavior is a combination of instant and acquired or learned behavior and dogs go through developmental stages just as people do. Dogs must learn by trial and error, they try something – if the outcome is rewarding they are more likely to do it again – if the outcome is unpleasant they are less likely to do it again. The

Chapter Five: Entertaining and Training Your Cockapoo

more often they have a pleasant outcome from a behavior the more rapidly they will learn to perform that behavior.

Chapter Five: Entertaining and Training Your Cockapoo

Chapter Six: Coat Types and Grooming

Grooming is very important to maintain your dog's coat texture and its skin. In this chapter you'll learn some tips on how to groom them and maintain their cuddly appearance while making sure that they are neat and tidy. We will also discuss the different coat types of cockapoo breeds so that you'll have an idea on the kind of coat your puppy might have. You'll also be given a list of the trimming tools you'll need to use if you want to do the grooming part yourself. This is another great bonding opportunity for you and your pet.

Chapter Six: Coat Types and Grooming

Different Cockapoo Coat Types

Cockapoos can have different coat types because their parent breeds are also bred from different combinations of designer dogs which is why it'll be really a surprise on what kind of coat or hair they're going to inherit. The four coat types typically seen in cockapoo puppies are a flat coat, a wavy or ringlet coat, a straight coat, and a curly or poodle - type coat. You're breeder can most likely know what kind of coat you're puppy is going to have as it grows up because they're the ones who bred the puppy in the first place. The coat will start to develop after a few weeks old to about a month; by then you can see if the puppy inherited the coat of a cocker spaniel breed or the poodle breed.

The cockapoos' coats usually have a soft, silky or dense texture. It can also be hypoallergenic since they're known for less dander or allergen and low – shedding qualities.

If the cockapoo inherited the poodle's coat qualities, then their coat will more likely be tight and curly, similarly if the pup inherited a cocker spaniel's coat qualities then you can expect their hair to be much straighter. The coats that are curly will more or less have low – shedding qualities, so you won't need to worry

Chapter Six: Coat Types and Grooming

about hairs being spread out in carpets or clothes. A curly hair doesn't need much brushing and grooming as well. But even if your dog doesn't shed that much they still need to be groomed weekly to prevent matting and to also maintain the coat's quality. Below are the four coat types of cockapoos:

Flat Coat

If you're cockapoo has developed a flat coat that means he has inherited more of the Cocker Spaniel's hair qualities. Flat coats are very low maintenance and they're also less likely to shed which means you don't need to clip it all the time.

Straight Coat

A loose wave type of hair is what makes up a straight coat among cockapoos. Your puppy may need regular grooming even if they are also low shedders. You just need to clip their hair at least three or four times in one year.

Wavy Ringlet Coat

If your cockapoo has a wavy ringlet coat type, you can expect him to look like a stuff teddy after about 2 months. However, they are quite high maintenance compare to other coat types and may need regular grooming to keep the coat from matting. The good news is that they don't shed as well.

Poodle Type Coat

As the name suggest, the coat of your puppy will have that tight kind of curly coat that is still non – shedding but he may need to be well groomed and maintained.

Grooming Your Cockapoo

Step 1: Start with the head. Comb your dog's hair back resembling a ponytail; put your fingers in an angle just about 1 inch off the base of your dog's skull. Then comb your entire dog's hair forward, and using your thinning shears, just cut an inverted V – shape above your dog's nose or between its eyes to expose the clean look of your dog's eye.

Step 2: Proceed to the eyes. Use a thinning shear or a straight scissors to avoid blood clots in the eye. Just carefully cut the corner of the eyes (about ½ inch down) both on the right and left side so that it is clean and well – blended

Chapter Six: Coat Types and Grooming

Step 3: Go down to its muzzle. Comb all the hair forward, and using your shears just cut the hair that are longer and seems irregular in its muzzle to its beard. This could shape your dog's nose and clean it up. Make sure to also clip the excess hairs or uneven hairs to tidy up your entire grooming process.

Step 4: Proceed to your dog's ear. Comb the hair in the ears downward. Using your straight scissors carefully cut the hair on the ears starting on its back portion until the tip of your cockapoo's ear. Cut the hair halfway down the ear and make sure that you don't cut it too far the ear and remove too much hair on its front portion. Don't forget to cut the hairs found on the tip of the ear and just curve it or shaped it

Step 5: Next is the body both in its back and tummy portion as well as its genital area. Start shaving the hair at the base of your pet's skull and work your way down from there – through its body, legs and down on its back as well as the sides and its tummy. Make your dog stand up and hold its front legs so you can easily access their bellies and private areas and do a haircut underneath. Make sure to carefully clip underneath its belly and in between the legs in its private parts. When clipping its bum area, be careful not to clip too short and not too far off the tail to not expose their rectum portion too much.

Step 6: Trim its tail. Once you get to the rump or your dog's back portion, you should make sure that you pull back its

Chapter Six: Coat Types and Grooming

tail inwards or between its legs before combing the back side to make sure you're smoothing out any curly hairs

Step 7: Proceed in trimming its paws and foot. Before cutting it up, you should first comb all the hair on its foot and around the paw pads downwards. Turn your dog's foot over to be able to cut that area. Be careful in cutting the hair on its paws as to not expose too much of the foot underneath. After doing that in all of its paws, make sure to brush the hair down again to straighten it out and also clip using scissors all the remaining hair around its paws to make sure that it is nice and clean.

Step 8: Clip its nails. Make sure to clip your dog's toenails with dog toenail clippers once every six or eight weeks. It will keep your dog's paws clean and healthy and will prevent him from scratching upon jumping up. Be sure not to cut their nails too close as this may hurt them.

Washing Your Pet

After you've gone over your cockapoo with the trimming part, your pup is now ready for bathing. The cockapoo doesn't need to be bathed frequently; you should only do it when he really needs it. If you bathe your dog too frequently it could cause his skin and coat to dry out. When you do bathe your dog, be sure to use dog-friendly shampoo that will be gentle on his skin. Here are some guidelines for bathing your cockapoo:

Step 1: Place a non-slip mat or towel on the bottom of your tub then fill it with a few inches of lukewarm water, then put your cockapoo in the tub and use a handheld sprayer or a container to wet down his coat as thoroughly as possible.

Step 2: Apply a small amount of your dog-friendly shampoo to your hand then work it into your cockapoo's coat, forming a thick soapy lather. Work the soap through the hair on your dog's neck, back, legs, chest and tail – avoid getting his ears, eyes, and nose wet.

Step 3: Thoroughly rinse away the soap using clean water until all traces have been removed. Use a damp washcloth to carefully clean the fur on your dog's head and face, if necessary, keeping the eyes and ears dry.

Step 4: Towel-dry your cockapoo using a large fluffy towel until you have removed as much moisture from his coat as possible.

Step 5: If it is cold out and your cockapoo is shivering, finish drying his coat using a hairdryer on the low heat setting. The most important thing to remember when bathing your cockapoo is that you must keep his ears dry. Wet ears are a breeding ground for bacteria and infection. The cockapoo doesn't have erect ears to allow plenty of airflow to the ear

Chapter Six: Coat Types and Grooming

canal, that's why there is a huge risk for ear infections so be very careful.

Chapter Seven: Feeding Your Cockapoo

Normally, once your new puppy arrives, the breeder where you got it from will leave you with some recommendations as to what kind of food that your puppy has been weaned into. As your new pup grows you'll find that he/she may like some certain types of brands or foods so it's entirely up to you and your pet if you'd like to change the diet that your pup has been accustomed to. This chapter will give you information on what type of diet is good for them and the things you should look out for when it comes to buying dog food brands.

Chapter Seven: Feeding Your Cockapoo

Feeding and Nutrition

When it comes to feeding your cockapoo pup, one of the first things to look out for is a food that contains a balanced amount of protein because some kibble and wet dog foods found in the supermarket only comes from animal derivatives or has a low percentage of protein.

Some keepers think that a relatively expensive price of food is a good indication of a high – quality dog food, though this could be sometimes true, pricing doesn't always translates to a nutritious dietary content. On the other hand, it doesn't mean that a cheaper price lacks a premium quality or is not that nutritious for your pet.

If you wanted to have an idea on how much the food will cost per bag or in a month, what you can do once you have picked a brand is to work out the cost per day or see how much the dog will consume in a month or how often you need to buy another bag to help you budget it or at least estimate the cost.

Some cockapoos prefer wet foods or meat that often comes in pouches or tins, what you can do is to try out different kinds of brands and food types for you to know which food/brand your puppy likes. Just make sure that you provide them with fresh water especially when you're feeding kibble or dry foods.

Chapter Seven: Feeding Your Cockapoo

Always ensure that there is a fresh bowl of drinking water available at all times when feeding kibble. In the next sections, we'll provide you a description of the most recommended dog food and brand for your cockapoo.

Understanding Dog Food labels

If you're just a first time dog keeper or a newbie at keeping pets in general, then buying a certain brand or deciding which commercial dog food to buy can be a lot of work! It's because first of all, there's a lot of brands and different type of foods in the shelves, you may not have an idea what to look out for, and the labels or ingredient found in each pack is sometimes confusing especially if you don't know what it means for your dog's nutritional needs. This is why you need to understand dog food labels and at least have an idea about it so you can make a wise decision.

What to Avoid

As mentioned earlier, the primary need of your dog is protein – a good percentage/content of protein. You may want to avoid food brands that contain soya ingredients because dogs have a hard time digesting it, which is why even if they are much cheaper, it's not good for your pet in the long run. You should also try avoiding dog foods containing lots of "unknown animals" or animal derivatives

Chapter Seven: Feeding Your Cockapoo

as well as vegetable derivatives. An animal derivative comes from animal/meat parts that contain proteins. Although it's cheaper, the problem is that it's more generic – which means that you don't exactly know where the meats are from and what parts are used. It's the same with vegetable derivatives; it often comes as a bulk of different veggies that are cheap but then again, you don't know if the vegetable had some residues or is already rotten when mixed with fillers.

You should also avoid dog foods that contain lots of "fillers." Fillers don't have nutritious elements in it – it usually comes in the form of cereals or grains. Aside from that, your dog might have wheat allergies or may develop one since these grain based foods are often times the cause of allergies in dogs. If you saw your cockapoo licking its paws, getting scratchy or developing ear infections, it may be because of the food containing too much filllers.

What You Should Look Out For

Here are the things you should look out for when checking out dog food labels or the nutritional list found at the back of the pack, this is based from the Feeding Regulation of 2005. The label must contain the following:

- The kind of dog breed for which the food was intended (ex: dog food for cockapoos – or breeds that are relatively similar)

Chapter Seven: Feeding Your Cockapoo

- It should also mention if the product is complete or complementary

- Has the proper feeding direction/instructions

- Must clearly mention where the meat came from or the vegetable content – not just generic names. (Ex: must be from chicken, beef or pork, not just "meat from animals" or "animal/vegetable derivatives" etc.).

- The ingredients at the back should be listed in a descending order of the weight. You should also consider the percentage of proteins (at least more than 4%), oils, fiber, fat, moisture (must not exceed 14%), and ash (it's the mineral content that is chemically determined upon burning the product).

- The ingredients list must also contain the level of preservatives, chemical, vitamins, antioxidants and other chemical names included in the food. The levels should have a clear indication of whether or not the raw food contains it or if it's only added.

Chapter Seven: Feeding Your Cockapoo

Nutritional Terms

Below are some nutritional terminologies often found in dog food labels/brands, we suggest that you be familiarize with it so that you can be aware once you're picking out the best food for your dog:

- **Meat:** Refers to a flesh of slaughtered animals either coming from animals like chicken, beef, pork, fish, turkey, lamb etc.

- **Animal Derivatives:** comes from different or unknown animal/meat parts that contain proteins and often includes beaks, feathers, hair, head and other internal organs.

- **Meat By – Products:** Clean flesh of animal parts that are not included in the meat including kidney, bone, fatty tissues, brain, liver, lungs, intestines, stomach, and blood but does not include teeth, hair, hooves or horns.

- **Poultry By – Products:** Similar to meat by – products, these are clean poultry parts coming from animals like hens, roosters, turkey etc. and includes the heads, internal organs and feet expect feathers.

- **Meal:** Contains whole and fresh meats from animals that are specified in the product label but does not contain any animal derivatives and also has an appropriate percentage of minerals and vitamins like calcium and phosphorus. A meal also has less moisture.

- **Brown Rice:** Unpolished rice that are a left over from kernels

- **BHA:** Artificial fat preservative

- **Ethoxyquin**: a chemical and artificial preservative used in preventing the dog food from being spoiled.

- **Tocopherols**: An example of this is Vitamin E; tocopherols are natural compounds or preservatives.

- **Animal Fat:** fats are essential to a healthy dog, and it's also a great source of nutrition for them more than vegetable fat. However, you should look out for a brand that specifies from which animal the fat came from. It's also cheap and your dog will surely love the brands containing animal fats.

- **Linoleic Acid**: Provides Omega 6 which is also important to the dog's diet.

Chapter Seven: Feeding Your Cockapoo

What is a BARF Diet?

Most keepers like to feed their dogs with a BARF (Bones and Raw Food) diet that contains meat, fruits, bones and veggies. The ideal amount to feed for adult dogs should be 2 – 3% of their body weight. You can start with 2% and gradually increase it because active breeds like cockapoos may need more (please also consult your vet regarding this). The ideal amount for puppies is 3% of their expected weight once they reached adulthood.

Feeding your puppy with bones is great because it can clean out your dog's teeth but make sure to not feed them with the bones of a cow or lamb's legs because they are quite dense and has the possibility to chip your dog's teeth. The ideal bones for your dog can come from pork, chicken, duck, lamb, rabbit etc.

The ideal ratio for a BARF diet is 80% protein and 10% for bones and for offal but of course adjust it depending on your dog's weight. If you think the feces of your dog is too hard then you might need to decrease the amount of bone, on the other hand, if they are very crumbly, you might need to slightly increase the bone amount you are feeding them. The offal should contain at least 5% liver. Avoid overfeeding them with liver because it contains vitamin A, and too much of it is not good for your pet.

Chapter Seven: Feeding Your Cockapoo

Protein

Protein is made up of amino acids and it is incredibly important for the growth and development of your cockapoo's tissues, organs, and cells. Dogs require animal-based proteins like fresh meat and meat meals because it provides them with the essential amino acids they cannot produce on their own. Plant-based proteins are less biologically valuable for your dog, though they are not essentially harmful. Here are some examples of proteins, offal and bones to feed your cockapoo:

Proteins Based Animals

- Chicken
- Beef
- Pork
- Duck
- Lamb
- Quail
- Turkey
- Pheasant
- Rabbit
- Pigeon
- Buffalo
- Raw Egg
- Salmon
- Oil Fish

Bones

- Duck (wings, spines, feet, neck, carcasses)
- Chicken (wings, spines, feet, neck, carcasses)
- Turkey (wings, carcasses, necks)

- Lamb (necks, breast, ribs, shanks)
- Beef (ribs)

Offal

- Kidney
- Pancreas
- Liver (5% only)
- Spleen

FAQs about Dog Feeding

Is feeding bones safe from?
Yes but just make sure that you never feed them with cooked bones because once the bones are cooked it can turn into a splinter which could choke your dog. Always provide them with raw bones that are suitable for their size. Don't give them with dense bones such as those from a cow's legs because it can cause a broken or cracked tooth. You should also supervise them when eating bones.

Is raw meat safe for my dog?
Yes, because even if it's raw they can still digest it because they have a stronger stomach acid and their short digestive tract can process food quickly compared to humans, which means that the raw meat is not left in their tummies for a long time.

Chapter Seven: Feeding Your Cockapoo

Is it okay to simultaneously feed my dog with kibble/commercial food and a raw diet?

It's not advisable to do this because it can cause confusion in their digestion. It could upset the stomach which can lead to digestive problems. What you can do is to feed them a certain type of diet for a period of time, and then change it to see if which kind it prefers.

Chapter Seven: Feeding Your Cockapoo

Chapter Eight: Breeding Your Cockapoos

Breeding cockapoos is not that easy especially for a novice breeder because you need to consider lots of factors. And just like being a responsible keeper, you need to make sure that you adhere to the breeding standards so that you can become a responsible breeder yourself. Keep in mind that it's not just about the money, for you to become a trustworthy dog breeder, you must be able to have passion for raising puppies and invest time and effort to make sure that the parent breed as well as their offspring is healthy.

Chapter Eight: Breeding Your Cockapoos

This chapter will shed light on whether you should become a breeder or just stay as a keeper. We'll give you some basic breeding process for cockapoos as well as some questions you need to ponder on before you decide if this is the road for you.

Reasons for Breeding

You can start becoming a hobby breeder or potentially a licensed breeder if you have the following qualities below:

- If you have prior experience about keeping cockapoos and have gained knowledge about the breed including its parents
- If you learned from someone who is a hobbyists/mentor or have closely worked with them when it comes to breeding cockapoos
- If you know how the different factors that needs to be considered through careful selection of the parent breeds especially in terms of the age, personality or temperament and health history for you to produce a healthy cockapoo
- If you already built a client based or if you have searched potential customers/prospective keepers already so that you won't struggle in selling them after being born

Chapter Eight: Breeding Your Cockapoos

- If you have considered the financial aspect of the breeding like the stud fees, the vet bills, the birthing materials, the space, and other costs involved in raising pups
- If you have the time to care for them and provide the newborns their needs as well as take care of the parents before and after giving birth
- If you are passionate about raising puppies or keeping dogs in general

Reasons for Not Considering Becoming a Breeder

If you only want to breed because you want to have another pet that has the same temperament as your dog.

If you find your household cockapoo pet very adorable, and you think you can replicate the same personality – think again. This is because there's no guarantee that the puppies will inherit your pet's qualities, obviously because they'll take on both the genes of their parents. Some breeders think that if they breed their pet with another similar breed, that the litter will duplicate the same traits – this is usually not the case. There'll be times when the puppies will not inherit anything similar to their mom and dad especially in terms of temperament, this is because

Chapter Eight: Breeding Your Cockapoos

the traits are usually learned and developed over time, not just inherited.

You just want to earn from it

Breeding dogs or any other animals for this matter is very expensive; sometimes it can even result in little to no profit! So if money is your only reason why you want to become a breeder, you may need to find a better motivation. There'll be lots of expenses starting from the mating of the breeds until the raising of the puppies. You have to take care of the travel expense of the dog and/or the accommodation if the stud is far away. You have to set aside money for vet fees including several medical tests, whelping materials, worming, vaccines, and emergency care just in case something will go wrong. You'll also need to spend money in advertising or marketing to get the word out that you are breeding pups.

Once the puppies are born, you'll have to buy more food, provide more space, buy more cleaning materials and even take care of the parents' health. Aside from all of that, you need to really monitor and supervise the dogs from the mating process up to the time the puppies are weaned. If only money, and not passion for this breed is your sole reason, it's probably best for you to not become the breeder.

Chapter Eight: Breeding Your Cockapoos

Your friends and relatives suggest you do it

You have to consider the fact that people's minds can change when it comes to acquiring a pet, which is why before deciding to become a breeder, you should have a plan B on how to handle the litter and take care of everything just in case you won't be able to sell the puppies for a period of time.

Many dogs and pups are ending up in rescue organizations because irresponsible breeders can't handle them anymore especially when they got no customers to sell to; sometimes they just abandon the animals anywhere just to get rid of them. Before deciding to sell or breed, you should also take the time to assess your potential customers even if they are friend of yours or a relative, for you to know if they are really committed and if they can provide the needs of the puppy.

You want your dog to have a litter before being spayed

Pregnancy, just like in humans, comes with risk. Sometimes bitches and their pups die during labor. There's also a risk of defects, illnesses or deformities that may require euthanasia. Dogs don't really care if they don't give birth to an offspring, and it's also not going to affect their health if they don't give birth before being spayed.

Chapter Eight: Breeding Your Cockapoos

Other Factors to Consider

Do you have what it takes to be a dog breeder?

Unfortunately, not everyone can become a dog breeder. You may think that being a keeper is similar to breeding them but it's not, breeding is a whole new different game. It's a risk to your pet, it will cost you big time, and you need to invest effort and time to take care of both the newborn puppies and the parent breed. You need to learn lots of things not just in terms of taking care of them but also during the birth process.

You need to be knowledgeable about the reproduction process of dogs so that if ever something goes wrong, you'll be able to aid your pet. You should also consider the possibility of keeping the unsold litters as your own pet which means that you need to provide the basic necessities for each of them including training and socialization. Financial capacity, time, passion, patience and commitment are needed before you become a real hobbyist or legit breeder. Do you have what it takes?

Is your home large enough to accommodate pets?

If you don't have space in your house to accommodate more than 2 or 3 dogs, then you should not

Chapter Eight: Breeding Your Cockapoos

consider becoming a breeder. The puppies as well as the parent breeds should have enough space to rest in and grow. Keep in mind that these pups come in litters – 4 to 6 puppies on average. Assuming that no one bought them, do you think they can have the space to roam around with once they grow up?

Can you dedicate your time for this practice?

You need to look after the mom and dad to supervise everything starting from their mating process until the weaning process once the puppy comes out, and until you give them to their new keepers. You should take the time to consider if you can fit breeding dogs into your lifestyle or social life. If you have a busy work life, and you wanted to become a breeder and just treat it as a side line because you think you can earn extra income then this practice may not be suitable for you. Breeding will need your full attention and focus.

Breeding Basics

It is important that you wait until the female reaches sexual maturity before you start breeding them. Most breeders recommend waiting until two years old to start breeding, though some dogs reach their full size even before

Chapter Eight: Breeding Your Cockapoos

they turn two years of age. This is an assurance that the dog is mature enough to physically carry and bear puppies, but it also provides enough time for any serious health problems to be spotted. Before six months of age, several dog organizations recommend having your dogs neutered or spayed. This is the time where the female dog experiences her first heat. The cycle is usually twenty days. What may be normal for one dog may differ from another.

If you want to increase your chances of a successful breeding, you need to keep track of your cockapoo's estrus cycle. Once your female reaches the point of ovulation, you can introduce her to the male dog and let nature take its course. Breeding behavior varies slightly from one breed to another, but you can expect the male dog to mount the female from behind after her heat cycle. If the breeding is successful, conception will occur and the gestation period will begin.

Once you see your dog having signs of congenital heart problems, it is more preferable to not breed her for a year or so. Dogs should only be bred preferably every other year. Consecutive conception and giving birth within a short span of time causes problems in her reproductive system and could result to a high level of loss in puppies. This is caused by different kinds of reasons, and can also happen in any breed not only among cockapoo as this happens more often in designer breeds.

Chapter Nine: Health and Safety

This chapter will focus on some safety reminder tips for your pet cockapoo for both the winter and summer season. We'll give you some guidelines on what kinds of activities you can do with your dog, the kind of clothing they may need to wear for protection, and how they can enjoy all year round without comprising their health and safety. As a pet keeper, it's your responsibility to ensure that your cockapoo is safe during harsh weather conditions and provide them with the things they need while having fun at the same time. If you learned some of these precautions, you can plan accordingly, keep your pup happy, and also dog – proof your house to avoid unforeseen circumstances as much as possible.

Chapter Nine: Health and Safety

Winter Care for Cockapoos

If you live in certain parts of the country where there is snow, then winter can be a fun season for your puppy. Your cockapoo will surely love to walk or play in the snow, not to mention the fact that you can dress them up during this cold season and just make them look more adorable. You can even purchase collars, tags or leash that lights up in the dark especially if you own a dark colored pup. While playing or walking your pet in the snow is fun for both of you, there's still some things you need to watch out for because the snow will definitely get attached to your dog's paws, coat, eyes, ears and its whole body. Sometimes if the ice lumps is mixed with other soil materials like gravel or debris, it can accumulate in your pet's paws and in between their toes which can be painful to remove.

Aside from the make sure that your dog don't eat the ice because sometimes it contains toxic chemicals and rock salt which can be bad for them when digested. It can also cause pancreatitis, dehydration and even liver failure. Never let your cockapoo ingest anti-freeze as well because it can be toxic for them. It's probably best to trim up the hairs in your dog's paws before you go out for a walk just to prevent the buildup of unnecessary debris on their toes or pads.

Chapter Nine: Health and Safety

You'll also probably need to groom your dog as the winter approaches because the cold condition along with them wearing a sweater or knitwear can cause the coat to be matted. Make sure to check for matting hot spots like their neck, armpit and legs area.

You should also try spraying either an olive oil or a coconut oil to your dog's body before going out into the snow, this is to prevent the ice from sticking on their coats while outside. Keep in mind that even if they wear winter clothes or layers of coat, they can still freeze up if they spend too much time outside especially if the weather is harsh.

Once you get home after walking in the snow, you may need to immerse your pet's legs in warm water to defrost any ice that gets attached to it. Make sure to check their paws and pads and remove any rock salt or debris if any. You can purchase a foot balm or coconut oil if their paws are dry or sore. Below is a list of items you can prepare for the winter season so that your cockapoo can be ready for the cold weather:

Mushers
This is a wax – based cream that is used to protect your pet's paws from ice, rocksalt, debris or sand. It can also help heal the wounds and rejuvenates the pads because it has Vitamin E to keep the feet healthy.

Chapter Nine: Health and Safety

Dog Boots

If the winter season in your location is quite extreme, then it's probably best to buy dog boots especially for dogs with sensitive paws. Your pet might be uncomfortable at first but if they'll eventually get used to it. It can serve as protection from icy debris and also from the cold ground.

Dog all in one suits

This may sound and even look strange for you, your dog and the people who are going to see your dog outside while wearing them, but it can help cover your pet's legs and feet during the cold season. It's like an overall clothing for your dog. You can purchase a variety of designs online or in retail stores.

Dog Coats

There are many types of dog coats like waterproof jackets, fleece, knitwear and a simple but thick sweater to cover them up and keep them warm. You can get bargain prices in online stores like Ebay or Amazon. The coats are often times measured from the dog's neck to its tail.

Colored collars, leash, tags etc.

This is particularly for pet owners who have dark colored cockapoos. During the winter and autumn season, the weather is gloomy and has long nights so if you decided to take your dog for a walk early in the morning or late at night, it's ideal to buy them reflective clothing so that you can see them in the dark.

Christmas Hazards

Make sure that your dog doesn't eat the ornaments in your Christmas tree. It can cause choking, internal blockage and cuts in its paws. Smashed ornaments must be removed immediately. It's probably best to place the decorations where your dog can't reach them.

Another thing that can be hazardous to your pet is the Christmas lights. Be careful when you're placing them and make sure that the wires, switch and plugs are out of reach because if unsupervised, your cockapoo may chew them or they can get electrocuted. Make sure that the wires have cable covering to prevent the dog from chewing it and causing trouble.

Chapter Nine: Health and Safety

Don't let your dog play with candles especially during Christmas season. Their curiosity with it can lead to unfortunate circumstances. Their tails can easily get caught on fire or may cause burns. The worst thing that can happen is that they'll knock it off and burn your house!

Make sure that your pets will not ingest Christmas plants that are poisonous like poinsetta, azaleas, holly, mistletoe and even pot pouri because even if your dog just ingested a small leaf, it can cause stomach problems or it can be toxic. Bring to the vet immediately if in case they chewed off poisonous plants.

Don't leave Christmas things like wrapping paper, ribbons, tinsel, strings or other gift materials because your pet can accidentally ingest them. It can cause lacerations and digestive problems if swallowed.

Christmas is the time for chocolates, alcohol, turkey, pudding, pies and other goodies but you have to keep in mind that these foods are harmful and toxic for your pet. Avoid feeding your pets with the following "Christmas foods" below:

Chocolate

Chocolate can cause vomiting and diarrhea, and if your dog eat lots of it, it can be fatal for them. Chocolate contains high levels of cocoa which are harmful for your pet.

Chapter Nine: Health and Safety

Alcoholic Drinks

Alcoholic drinks is not tolerated by the dog's body; it will have the same effect just as with humans like loss of coordination, vomiting or diarrhea but the effect will be much quicker and can also be fatal.

Turkey Bones or Cooked Bones

As mentioned in the feeding chapter, never feed your cockapoo with cooked bones – turkey bones for this matter unless they are raw. Cooked bones can easily be cracked and ingested but it can puncture your dog's intestinal tract or choke them up. Don't feed them your left over dinner but you can give them a few slices of the turkey meat.

Pies and Pudding

The raisins found in pies or pudding is toxic for dogs because it can cause kidney failure and fatality. Bring to the vet immediately. Letting them eat a pie or pudding is not entirely bad but make sure that the ingredients you used are not harmful for your dog.

Chapter Nine: Health and Safety

Summer Care for Cockapoos

Summer is the time for beaches, outdoor activities, and lots of fun! Your cockapoo will surely look forward to this season because he can play outside almost all the time. However, you still need to take care of them to keep them safe. You might also want to keep them cool to prevent heat strokes or fatigue because of the hot weather.

Here are some tips to ensure that your cockapoo will have a fun – filled summer:

- Don't leave your pet inside your car during summer (unless of course the aircon is on) because the temperature inside can be hotter than the condition outside. Your dog may overheat because they can't cool themselves which can then lead to brain damage, heat stroke or death.

- If you're travelling in your car, make sure that you have car shades to help protect your dog in the sun's heat/UV rays.

- For cockapoos that are light in color, you may want to put on sunscreen to protect them especially vulnerable parts like their muzzle, ears, and lips. You

Chapter Nine: Health and Safety

can consult your vet on what brand is suited for your dog or safe for them because they could lick it.

- As much as possible, don't take your dog out for a walk if the temperature outside is really hot. You should take them out early in the morning (around 6 to 9 am), late in the afternoon (around 5 pm onwards) or at night to prevent heat stroke or overexposure under the sun's heat. If possible, walk them out in areas where there's a shade.

- Make sure that your cockapoo's coat is all groomed up and short during summer because tangled coats can cause the heat to be trapped in their body making them feel uncomfortable and hot.

- Always have fresh or cold water available for your dog if you're going to walk him out, travel with him or just generally let him play around your house during the hot season. Your dog will need to be hydrated at all times so make sure that their water bowls are always refilled as they will drink more.

- Even if summer is equal to lots of playtime and fun, make sure that the activities that your dog will be engaged in are monitored and supervise because they can easily exhaust themselves during the hot weather

Chapter Nine: Health and Safety

without them knowing it. Let them take a break, and take the home for a rest if you see that they're panting or really tired already.

- Just like during the winter season, the sun can pretty much heat up the roads and pavements so be mindful of your cockapoo's paws because the heated roads can cause blisters.

- Make sure that the roads they're going to be walking on are shaded so that the road is not that hot for their paws.

- As much as possible, don't get your dog in crowded places because it can be stressful for them especially if the temperature is humid.

- If you're going to have barbecue parties over your house, ensure that the cooking materials like grills, gas, flames or other hazardous things are out of reach. Don't let them eat lots of fatty foods as well.

- Summer is also the time to do gardening chores but be mindful of the pesticides you're going to use because it can be toxic for your dog. Ensure that the plants are non – toxic as well, and keep the dangerous

Chapter Nine: Health and Safety

gardening tools out of reach to prevent any serious injury.

- If you're going to take your dog out for a swim, make sure that precautions are taken. Make sure that the level of water is not too deep for your dog to prevent drowning or other injury. Also watch out for algae or other dangerous sea creatures like jellyfish because they can sting your dog as well. You also have to ensure that the pool, lake or any body of water that your dog is going to splash into is not contaminated by harmful chemicals or pesticides as this may cause skin irritation and other illnesses if ingested.

- After swimming, give your dog a bath as soon as possible to ensure that they're clean. Thoroughly dry up their ears to avoid being damp because if not, it can become a breeding ground for bacteria.

- Bring your dog to the vet as soon as possible if they'll experience water intoxication

Chapter Nine: Health and Safety

Health Issues

Just like any other designer breeds, cockapoos are pre-dispose to certain hereditary illnesses that are similar to their Poodle and Cocker Spaniel parent breeds. If you want to know what potential diseases your pup can acquire, it's ideal that you let them undergo through different medical tests to screen if they have a condition. You may also want to check the medical tests of your pup's parent breed because this will tell you the kind of health your puppy could potentially inherited.

Cockapoos usually suffer from degenerative eye condition. This is something that is inherited from their parents which is why breeders screen their dogs annually to check if their eyes are in good condition. Some conditions like patellar luxation, hip dysplasia, obesity, and other chronic illnesses are either developed overtime due to bad health habits or can also be caused by recessive genes. Whatever it may be, it's always important to have your dog regularly checked up by their vet especially during their puppy years to prevent potential fatal diseases from worsening.

Chapter Ten: Care Sheet and Summary

Now that you have finished reading this book, it's time to apply what you've learned and experience what it's really like to become a responsible cockapoo keeper. It may not be easy but it's going to be worth it. At the end of the day, you'll surely have a great time with your pet and he'll form a close bond with your family as well. In this chapter, we will give you a quick summary of the major points you need to remember that was discussed in this book. A quick glance can be of help if you are in a hurry or if you simply wanted to review something important. Good luck and may you and your cockapoo live happily together!

Chapter Ten: Care Sheet and Summary

Cockapoos Inside Out!

Origin: United States

Pedigree: crossbreed of American/English Cocker Spaniel and Poodle

Breed Size/Type: Maxi, Mini, Toy and Teacup breed

Body Type and Appearance: These dogs have relatively small and broad heads have dropped ears that are small, well - set and furry, and they are available in many colors.

Height: Maxi or Standard Cockapoo can reach 15 inches; Mini cockapoos are typically 11 to 14 inches tall; Teacups only stand less than 10 inches while toy breeds is between 10 and 11 inches tall.

Weight: They can be classified as miniature (13 – 18 lbs.) and maxi cockapoos (19 lbs.), toy (7 – 12 lbs.), and also teacup breed (less than 6 lbs.) which is kind of similar to the different poodle types.

Coat Length: around 4 – 6 inches of either flat, straight, wavy or poodle like coat

Coat Texture: dense, silky, soft fur

Color: Black, Sable, Parti, Chocolate, Phantom, Buff, Roan, Apricot, White, Red, and Cream plus other range of colors.

Chapter Ten: Care Sheet and Summary

Ears: dropped ears, small

Tail: short to medium - length

Temperament: sociable, friendly, trainable, obedient, active, playful, loyal, affectionate

Strangers: super friendly around strangers

Other Dogs: generally loves to play with other dogs if properly trained and socialized

Other Pets: friendly with other pets including cats

Training: intelligent, obedient, and easily trained

Exercise Needs: regular amount of exercise is needed

Health Conditions: maybe prone minor illnesses like ear infections (due to their dropped ears), parasites, cataracts, knee dislocation and other internal diseases. .

Lifespan: average 14 – 18 years

Cockapoos as Pets

Questions to Consider Before Keeping Cockapoos as Pets

- Can you provide long term commitment?
- Do you have patience to train them?
- Grooming and coat maintenance can cost a lot; do you have the budget and time?

Chapter Ten: Care Sheet and Summary

- Can you keep up with their energy?
- Can you cover possible health treatments or can you avail a pet insurance?
- Cockapoos craves attention; can you give them your full commitment?
- Do you want a cockapoo because you've been told that they are hypoallergenic?
- Do you just want a cockapoo because they don't molt or just because they are cute?
- Do you want a cockapoo because you think they are classy?
- Do you want a cockapoo because you think they don't get sick?
- Can you spend time with them even if you work full time?

Finding a Reputable Breeder

Hobby Breeder vs. Licensed Breeder

- Hobbyists are not permitted to breed more than 4 litters in a year which is why availability of puppies can be restricted. On the other hand licensed breeders approved by a certain organization or someone who has been issued with a certificate can breed more than

Chapter Ten: Care Sheet and Summary

four litters in a year which means that they can have puppies all year round and that you are less likely to be put into the waiting list.

Questions to ask:

- How old are the puppies (that they're going to sell to you)?
- Are the parents of dogs are healthy, can you prove it?
- Can the parents of the pups be viewed?
- How old are the parents and how many litters did the mom produced this year?
- Are the pups being regularly wormed?
- Are the puppies vaccinated and treated for fleas?
- Are the puppies raised indoors?
- Are the puppies' microchipped?
- Do you offer after sale support?
- Can you provide a contract?
- Does the puppy have a free insurance?
- Will the puppy come home with a "puppy pack"?
- Do you require a deposit?
- Notice if the breeder is also asking you questions.

Chapter Ten: Care Sheet and Summary

Puppy Preparation

Crate: The ideal crate size for puppy cockapoos is around 36 inches, this is to ensure that your puppy have an ample space where he/she can move around comfortably and sleep well.

Bedding: You need not to spend a lot of money in buying a bed because they will surely outgrow it overtime. It's ideal to buy a vet bed because it's very easy to wash; it's cozy, soft, puppy proof and has variety of colors and designs that will surely make your cockapoo happy.

Puppy Pads: It's cheap and it could easily toilet train your puppy

Toys: You should provide at least 3 or more dog toys to stimulate your cockapoo

Kitchen Roll: Kitchen roll is used so that the urine or poo of your puppy will not retain its smell

Water Dishes and Food Bowls: A stainless food and water dishes are also ideal because it's durable and also quite easy to clean.

Poo Bags: use to segregate their poo in your garbage.

Chapter Ten: Care Sheet and Summary

Entertaining and Socializing Your Cockapoo

Games for Your Cockapoos

- Hide The Treat!
- Blow Up that Balloon!
- Sand Pit
- Trick or Treats?
- Puzzle Box
- Bubbles
- Swimming
- Bobbing Balls

Socialization Tips

- Mingle your puppy to different kinds of people
- Introduce your puppy to children of different ages.
- You should also expose your cockapoo to various appliances and tools around the house

Coat Types and Grooming

Flat Coat: Flat coats are very low maintenance and they're also less likely to shed which means you don't need to clip it all the time.

Straight Coat: A loose wave type of hair is what makes up a straight coat among cockapoos.

Chapter Ten: Care Sheet and Summary

Wavy Ringlet Coat: They are quite high maintenance compare to other coat types and may need regular grooming to keep the coat from matting

Poodle Type Coat: A tight kind of curly coat that is still non – shedding. It may need to be well groomed and maintained

Washing Your Cockapoo

Step 1: Place a non-slip mat or towel on the bottom of your tub then fill it with a few inches of lukewarm water.

Step 2: Apply a small amount of your dog-friendly shampoo to your hand then work it into your cockapoo's coat, forming a thick soapy lather.

Step 3: Thoroughly rinse away the soap using clean water until all traces have been removed.

Step 4: Towel-dry your cockapoo using a large fluffy towel

Step 5: Finish drying his coat using a hairdryer on the low heat setting.

Chapter Ten: Care Sheet and Summary

Feeding Your Cockapoo

Feeding and Nutrition

- Offer a food that contains a balanced amount of protein
- Some cockapoos prefer wet foods or meat that often comes in pouches or tins, what you can do is to try out different kinds of brands and food types for you to know which food/brand your puppy likes.
- Always ensure that there is a fresh bowl of drinking water available at all times when feeding kibble.

Understanding Dog Food labels

What to Avoid:

- You may want to avoid food brands that contain soya ingredients
- You should also try avoiding dog foods containing lots of "unknown animals" or animal derivatives as well as vegetable derivatives.
- You should also avoid dog foods that contain lots of fillers

Chapter Ten: Care Sheet and Summary

What You Should Look Out For

- The kind of dog breed for which the food was intended
- Has the proper feeding direction/instructions
- Must clearly mention where the meat came from or the vegetable content – not just generic names.
- The ingredients list must also contain the level of preservatives, chemical, vitamins, antioxidants and other chemical names included in the food.

Breeding Your Cockapoos

Reasons for Breeding

- If you have prior experience about keeping cockapoos
- If you know how the different factors that needs to be considered
- If you already built a client based or if you have searched potential customers/prospective keepers

Reasons for Not Considering Becoming a Breeder

- If you only want to breed because you want to have another pet that has the same temperament as your dog.
- You just want to earn from it
- You want your dog to have a litter before being spayed

Chapter Ten: Care Sheet and Summary

Health and Safety

Winter Care for Cockapoos

- Keep in mind the snow and prevent it from getting attached to your dog's paws, coat, eyes, ears and its whole body. It can accumulate in your pet's paws and in between their toes which can be painful to remove.
- Make sure that your dog doesn't eat the ice because sometimes it contains toxic chemicals and rock salt which can be bad for them when digested.
- After walking in the snow, you may need to immerse your pet's legs in warm water to defrost any ice that gets attached to it

Summer Care for Cockapoos

- Always have fresh or cold water available for your dog
- For cockapoos that are light in color, you may want to put on sunscreen to protect them especially vulnerable parts like their muzzle, ears, and lips.
- Make sure that your cockapoo's coat is all groomed up and short during summer

Chapter Ten: Care Sheet and Summary

Health Issues

- Cockapoos usually suffer from degenerative eye condition. This is something that is inherited from their parents which is why breeders screen their dogs annually to check if their eyes are in good condition.

- Some conditions like patellar luxation, hip dysplasia, obesity, and other chronic illnesses are either developed overtime due to bad health habits or can also be caused by recessive genes.

Glossary of Dog Terms

AKC – abbreviation for American Kennel Club; it is the biggest dog registry organization in America

Almond Eye – Refers to an elongated eye shape. It appears as an oblong shape and not roundish or circular

Apple Head – A skull that has a round-shaped

Balance – It is a jargon show term which refers to the dog's movement when standing and/or walking that also projects a harmonious image.

Beard – Refers to the long, and/or thick hair in the underjaw of dogs

Best in Show – A show term that refers to a form of recognition; it is given to the undefeated dog during competitions.

Bitch – A female dog

Bite – It is when the upper and lower teeth of the dog touches as it closes its jaws; it can either be a level bite, undershot bite, scissors, and overshot bite.

Blaze – It is a white stripe that can be found in the center of the face between the dog's eyes

Board – To house, feed, and care for a dog for a fee

Breed – a race of dogs that have a common gene pool or a dog's characterization based on its appearance, function or personality.

Breed Standard – It is a document that describes the official standard from a certain dog registry or organization that specifies the appearance, movement and the dog's behavior.

Buff – It is a white to gold coloring

Clip – A term that refers in cutting the coat for some breeds

Coat – Has two types; an outer coat and an undercoat (or double coat). It refers to the skin or fur of the dog breed

Condition – The condition of a dog in terms of its coat, body appearance, temperament, and overall behavior.

Crate – Similar to a cage or kennel; use to transport dogs and serves as a shelter

Crossbreed (Hybrid) – A dog having a sire and the offspring of two different dog breeds. These types of dog cannot be officially registered in some dog registry because it is not purebred.

Dam (bitch) – The female parent of a dog

Drop Ear – It refers to the kind of ear that folds over and hangs down. It is neither prick nor erect

Dock Tail – A shorten form of tail in dogs. Sometimes owners also surgically cut their dog's tail, making it shorter or docked.

Fancier – A person interested in a particular dog breed.

Feathering – It is the long hair in the dog's tail, legs, body or ears

Groom – Refers to the act of brushing, trimming, or combing the dog's fur or skin making the coat neat in appearance

Heel – A command to dogs which means to stay close by the owner's side

Hip Dysplasia – A condition characterized by the abnormal formation of the hip joint

Inbreeding – The breeding of two closely related dogs of one breed

Kennel – Refers to the dog's enclosure

Litter – Refers to the group of puppies born at the same time

Markings – A pattern or flashes of color on a dog's coat

Mask – The darkish part on the dog's foreface

Mate – The act of sexing a male dog and a female dog to produce puppies

Neuter – To castrate a male dog or spay a female dog or remove their reproductive system to avoid unwanted pregnancies.

Pads – The thick skin at the bottom of a dog's foot or paw.

Parti-Color – A coloration of a dog's coat consisting of two or more definite, well-broken colors; one of the colors must be white

Pedigree – It refers to the record of a dog's genealogy that goes back to its parents, grandparents, and ancestors.

Pied – Refers to a coloration consisting of white patches and another color

Prick Ear – Ear that is carried erect, usually pointed at the tip of the ear

Puppy – A dog under 12 months of age; a newborn dog

Purebred – A dog that came from the same pedigree or breed group

Saddle – Colored markings in the shape of a saddle over the back; colors may vary

Shedding – The natural process whereby old hair falls off the dog's body as it is replaced by new hair growth.

Sire – The dog's father or male parent

Smooth Coat – close – lying short hairs on the dog's skin

Spay – The surgical procedure to remove the reproductive system of a female dog making her incapable of breeding

Trim – To pluck or clip a dog's hair

Undercoat – Located under the longer outer coat; usually soft and silky.

Wean – Refers to a process in which puppies transition from drinking colostrum from their mom's milk to eating dog foods.

Whelping – Happens during the labor of a pregnant bitch

Photo Credits

Page 1 Photo by user Keith Williams via Flickr.com, https://www.flickr.com/photos/keithmwilliams/35320138500/

Page 5 Photo by user Cindy Devin via Flickr.com, https://www.flickr.com/photos/cindydevin/16610195568/

Page 13 Photo by user Nuwandalice via Flickr.com, https://www.flickr.com/photos/nuwandalice/13745259773/

Page 23 Photo by user chris id via Flickr.com, https://www.flickr.com/photos/chris_jd/6657629317/

Page 35 Photo by user John W via Flickr.com, https://www.flickr.com/photos/st3wy/7530498204/

Page 47 Photo by user Greg Dunlap via Flickr.com, https://www.flickr.com/photos/heyrocker/129202590/

Page 56 Photo by user Ray Larabie via Flickr.com, https://www.flickr.com/photos/27117620@N06/5992470306/

Page 65 Photo by user Jason Meredith via Flickr.com, https://www.flickr.com/photos/merfam/7054918711/

Page 76 Photo by user John W via Flickr.com,
https://www.flickr.com/photos/st3wy/7052339067/

Page 85 Photo by user Justin Charles via Flickr.com,
https://www.flickr.com/photos/justincharles/2135810809/

Page 97 Photo by user Nuwandalice via Flickr.com,
https://www.flickr.com/photos/nuwandalice/15388408154/

References

"Cockapoo" – Dogtime.com
http://dogtime.com/dog-breeds/cockapoo#/slide/1

"Cockapoo Basics" PetGuide.com
http://www.petguide.com/breeds/dog/cockapoo/

"Feeding a Cockapoo" - CockapooClubGB.co.uk
http://www.cockapooclubgb.co.uk/feeding.html

"Grooming" - CockapooClubGB.co.uk
http://www.cockapooclubgb.co.uk/grooming.html

"Keeping your Cockapoo entertained!" - CockapooOwners-Club.org.uk
http://www.cockapooowners-club.org.uk/entertaining-your-cockapoo.html

"Puppy Preparation" - CockapooOwners-Club.org.uk
http://www.cockapooowners-club.org.uk/puppy-preparation.html

"Should I Breed?" - CockapooOwners-Club.org.uk

http://www.cockapooowners-club.org.uk/should-i-breed.html

"Summer Care" - CockapooOwners-Club.org.uk
http://www.cockapooowners-club.org.uk/summer-care.html

"Taking Puppy Home" - CockapooOwners-Club.org.uk
http://www.cockapooclubgb.co.uk/taking-puppy-home.html

"Thinking Of Buying A Cockapoo Puppy?" Cockapoo.me
http://cockapoo.me

"Winter Care" - CockapooOwners-Club.org.uk
http://www.cockapooowners-club.org.uk/winter-care.html

Feeding Baby
Cynthia Cherry
978-1941070000

Axolotl
Lolly Brown
978-0989658430

Dysautonomia, POTS
Syndrome
Frederick Earlstein
978-0989658485

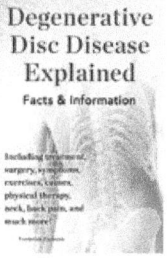

Degenerative Disc
Disease Explained
Frederick Earlstein
978-0989658485

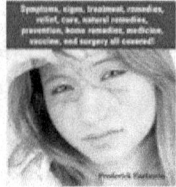

Sinusitis, Hay Fever,
Allergic Rhinitis Explained
Frederick Earlstein
978-1941070024

Wicca
Riley Star
978-1941070130

Zombie Apocalypse
Rex Cutty
978-1941070154

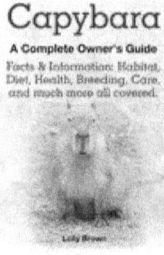

Capybara
Lolly Brown
978-1941070062

Eels As Pets
Lolly Brown
978-1941070167

Scabies and Lice Explained
Frederick Earlstein
978-1941070017

Saltwater Fish As Pets
Lolly Brown
978-0989658461

Torticollis Explained
Frederick Earlstein
978-1941070055

Kennel Cough
Lolly Brown
978-0989658409

Physiotherapist, Physical Therapist
Christopher Wright
978-0989658492

Rats, Mice, and Dormice As Pets
Lolly Brown
978-1941070079

Wallaby and Wallaroo Care
Lolly Brown
978-1941070031

Bodybuilding Supplements
Explained
Jon Shelton
978-1941070239

Demonology
Riley Star
978-19401070314

Pigeon Racing
Lolly Brown
978-1941070307

Dwarf Hamster
Lolly Brown
978-1941070390

Cryptozoology
Rex Cutty
978-1941070406

Eye Strain
Frederick Earlstein
978-1941070369

Inez The Miniature Elephant
Asher Ray
978-1941070353

Vampire Apocalypse
Rex Cutty
978-1941070321

www.ingramcontent.com/pod-product-compliance
Lightning Source LLC
LaVergne TN
LVHW051645080426
835511LV00016B/2499